Advice *for my* Daughter

Relationship and Life Advice that She Won't Take, But Maybe You Will

KATIE LARSON

ADVICE TO MY DAUGHTER

Relationship and Life Advice that She Won't Take, But Maybe You Will

Copyright © 2019 by Katie Larson
All rights reserved.
ISBN- 978-0-578-61587-5 in print form

No part of this publication may be reproduced, stored in a retrieval system or transmitted in any way without the prior permission of the author except as provided by the USA copyright law.

Table of Contents

Dedication — 5
Introduction — 6

Part I: Advice for Dealing with Boys — 8

Chapter 1: Do Not Chase a Guy — 9
Chapter 2: Boys Separate Emotions and Physical Activity — 11
Chapter 3: Sometimes You Get Dumped — 17
Chapter 4: Cry with Family and Good Friends — 21
Chapter 5: Your World is Bigger Than Him — 24
Chapter 6: Give Your Boyfriend Space — 28
Chapter 7: Stay Away from Controlling Relationships — 31
Chapter 8: Keep Your Relationships on Social Media Light — 34
Chapter 9: Be Single in College — 37
Chapter 10: Communicate What You Want — 39

PART II: ADVICE for Dealing with Girl Friends — 43

Chapter 11: Understand Girls — 44
Chapter 12: Try to Always Be Fair and Kind to Your Friends — 47
Chapter 13: Don't Let a Girl Friend Put You Down — 50
Chapter 14: Learn Which Friends You Can Trust — 53
Chapter 15: Don't Be Angry at a Friend for Talking Behind Your Back When You Have Done the Same — 55
Chapter 16: All People are So Different — 58

Chapter 17: Be Judgment Free   60

Chapter 18: Travel with Your Girlfriends Before Settling Down   62

Part III: Advice for Life   65

Chapter 19: Always Be Kind   66

Chapter 20: Choose Work That Makes You Happy and Try Your Best   68

Chapter 21: Keep Social Media Positive   71

Chapter 22: Keep Politics and Religion Out of Social Functions   73

Chapter 23: Do Not Be a Doormat   75

Chapter 24: Laugh at Yourself Often   77

Chapter 25: Live on Your Own Before You Live with a Boy   80

Chapter 26: Stay Classy and Educated on Social Media (and In Public)   83

Chapter 27: You are Not Better Than Anyone and No One is Better Than You   86

Chapter 28: If You Do Not Like Something, Do Not Become It   89

Chapter 29: Don't Make Excuses   92

Chapter 30: Protect Yourself   94

Chapter 31: Live in the Moment   97

Acknowledgements   100

Dedication

This is dedicated to my smart, courageous, brave, beautiful, creative, kind, and fabulous daughter, Elle. May you always know your worth.

This is also dedicated to all the young women in my life, former students, friends, nieces, and cousins. I hope this finds you well.

Introduction

I have a daughter that I want to protect with every ounce of my being. I am aware that advice from your own mom is lame and usually not taken. It does not mean that I won't share advice anyway. Since there is a good chance she will not take my advice, I decided to share it with the world. My hope is that other young women may find and take this advice.

This all started on July 7, 2012. Elle was just two years old. I started a document of advice and added to it over the years. It is important that I share the date I started this advice because I do not want her to think my advice comes from anything she has done thus far. If my daughter takes half of this advice, I will be happy. I know she has heard some of this before, but it bears repeating.

Let me share that I am not an expert in psychology or sociology. I am purely writing advice based off my observations and experiences. Some advice was given to me as well. I may not be an expert, but I do believe that I know what I am talking about.

I am intrigued by psychology and human behavior. I always wonder why people do what they do. In undergrad, I minored in psychology. Again this does not make me an expert. I have just been fascinated by psychology.

Another important thing to mention is that I watch too much TV. Most of it is reality TV. Because of this, I have seen patterns in human behavior. I have observed what is going well and what never goes well. I am at the point that I can predict what the reality personality will do next.

My goal is to help young women. Personally, I believe your 20s are the hardest years. Figuring out how to be an adult and growing up is hard. This advice comes from the heart. All of this advice is advice your own mom would give you as well, you may just listen more because I am not your mom.

It is written in three parts. You can read it all at once, or read the parts that are the hardest for you at the moment. I think you should read it when you are in your teens and again when you are in your 20s. Then you should probably read it again later too. We all could use some reminders in life. I read personal development books regularly. To each of you reading this, I love you and appreciate you.

Part 1: Advice for Dealing with Boys

"Because of his hormones, he only has three emotions: crabby, hungry, and horny."- Sherry Argov, *Why Men Love Bitches: Doormat to Dreamgirl-A Woman's Guide to Holding Her Own in a Relationship*

Chapter 1: Do Not Chase a Guy

You will like many boys in your life. Sometimes the emotions will be so strong. Do yourself a favor and never go after them. If a boy likes you, you will know. If you pursue him, odds are he will back away. I know this is easier said than done, so instead of focusing on the boy, focus on yourself and your friends.

I cannot tell you how many boys I liked. Some liked me back and others did not. Sometimes it sucked and that was ok. Each experience and heartache taught me something and helped me grow.

A boy liking you does not validate your worth. When I was younger and probably up until I started dating your dad, I unconsciously valued my worth on whether a guy liked me or not. That is pretty sad. If you love yourself and value yourself, guys and people will be attracted to that. Again: someone liking you does not give you worth.

To get into the psychology and sociology of life, males tend to be the chasers. I read that because, in the beginning of time, males were the hunters and gatherers, they are more wired to be the chasers. Boys are turned off by being chased. Going after a boy you like is called chasing. No one wants to be a chaser. You will feel the same at times. Someone will like you and you will not return the feelings. You will eventually get annoyed if he keeps pursuing you. Unrequited love is a thing. It can and it will go both ways.

You can never make someone like you; so don't try. They will like you or they will not. The world will still spin and you will still be amazing. It is more important to like yourself than to have a boy like you.

I am not alone in this belief. There is a book by Greg Behrendt and Liz Tuccillo, *He's Just Not That Into You*. It has great insight into this topic. Read this and trust me when I give you my wisdom. This book was turned into a hit movie.

Another book is written by Sherry Argov, *Why Men Love Bitches*. This book also validates my statement. A friend told me to read it, I loved it immediately. I shared it with all my friends, it has great advice. In fact, at my baby shower, Aunt Bridgett got you the book.

You are probably thinking, great but now what do I do instead. Well, I have thought of a few things to do instead of chasing a boy. First, you need to figure out what you enjoy. This is not the easiest thing to do. I remember job interviews or applications asking for my hobbies. I don't know, does watching TV and hanging with friends count as a hobby? This will require you to focus on yourself. When are you the happiest? Where are you the happiest? No relationship can make you happy, you need to find happiness from within.

Second, work on yourself. I remember not loving myself. Teen years are so lonely. I constantly compared myself to others. This must stop. Stop comparing yourself to anyone. You can work on yourself by being the healthiest you can be. Notice I did not say the skinniest. You need to be healthy and strong. Drink lots of water daily. Eat your vegetables. Move your body.

Finally, try something new. Take a class that may interest you. Maybe you want to take a photography class or a social media class. Maybe you want to take a Zumba class or a yoga class. This will help you find a hobby or a new lifestyle.

Now I will get personal on how this advice has worked for me. Your dad pursed me. I did not follow him around or try to get him to like me. Now there were guys in my life before your dad. There were times when I liked someone and pursued him and he did not return the same feelings. Relationships will come, be patient and do not go chasing them. The biggest piece of advice on this topic is not to focus on boys too much. Relationships can be fun but they are not everything.

Your dad finally asked me out on a date. We were friends for so long. If I were to ask him out first, he probably would have been less attracted to me. Then where would we be?

Chapter 2: Boys Separate Emotions and Physical Activity

There will be times that you feel pressured to do more physically. Never do more than you are ready for, and then still do less. Getting more physical with a boy, will not make him like you more. There will be times that you are both exploring each other together and other times where he just wants to see how far he can go with you.

Girls are driven by emotions more than boys. Boys are driven by hormones and sex. They will always go further. Do not cave and give in. Recognize the huge difference here. Emotions do not equate intimate activity.

There is a television show that came out in the last 10 years. It is Called 16 and Pregnant. In every case, a girl has gotten pregnant in her teens. She then had to make an impossible decision. In all the episodes when she wanted to give the baby up for adoption, the guy talked her out of it. That guy never stayed around after the baby was born. The show followed the girl for 6 weeks. In those six weeks, the guy was gone. She was ALWAYS left taking care of the baby that she wasn't ready for.

No teen should have to make this life decision, especially when deciding what to wear on picture day is hard enough. Raising a baby is not easy. Teen life is not easy. You struggle to fit in or stand out. You are not capable of solely taking care of yourself at this age. Live high school life. For this short amount of time let your biggest stress be picking out the right clothes to go out. That is enough to deal with at this age.

I have known girls that have had children at a young age. A child is a blessing but it is hard to realize that when you are still a child yourself. You will miss out on so many childhood and teen experiences. No matter what, getting pregnant as a teen becomes the girl's responsibility. The guy can go about his life without all the hormones and body changes. You do not get that luxury. I loved high school and college and it would have been so much more difficult to be responsible for another life when I was not capable of taking care of myself.

I was 30, married, and had a career when I had you. It was still so difficult and emotional. My hormones were all over the place. It is probably the scariest thing in the world, realizing that I was responsible for another life. So wait and be sure you are ready. Always protect yourself.

Another show that I binge-watched was Jersey Shore. It was crazy, funny, entertaining, and reality. The guys went out and looked for girls that were DTF. I will share that acronym with you later. They would bring girls home and never talk to them again. You don't want to be that girl that fulfilled a 15-minute need. They would call the girls a cab and send them home. Another quote that I read was: Strive to be someone's Sunday afternoon, not his Saturday night.

Love and physical activity are not interchangeable. They never will be. Enjoy all the emotions and the ride. Never assume anyone feels the same way as you. Never assume sleeping with a boy means he loves you. If you can remember this, it will help you.

You need to protect yourself. First, you need to be strong enough to say no. Be honest and upfront. If you are not ready to go further, make that clear. Do not let his frustration change your mind. It is your body and life. It is YOUR BODY and YOUR LIFE, not his. Just because you are in love with someone, does not mean you have to sleep with that person.

Let me share this story with you. When I was pregnant with you, I would get just a little nauseous in the morning. It wasn't so bad. My friend would actually throw up everyday for the nine months with each pregnancy. Being pregnant is different for everyone. I personally did not love it. Once my belly started growing my vagina started hurting. It was extremely painful. I would get shooting pains. Then I found out I had a varicose vein on my vagina. I never had a varicose vein before. It is a raised large vein that has a lot of blood flow. The pressure caused it. In what world is it fair that women have to go through all of this. You don't want to go through this too early.

Second, make sure you are always protected. Not just for pregnancy, but also for STDs. Who cares if the guy doesn't like condoms? Would he like to carry a baby for nine months and then go through labor and delivery? Men that have worn belts, to imitate contractions, could not handle the pain. Men can't handle getting a cold. Make him wear a condom each and every time. The younger you are, the more fertile you are. Do not think for one second that it won't happen to you. It can and it will. Also, don't just rely on the pill. That only helps prevent pregnancy if taken regularly and consistently. Your uncle Kevin was conceived while Nana was on the pill. I have known other people that have also gotten pregnant while taking birth control. It is not 100% effective. So use multiple forms of protection or simply abstain. Besides creating a life, you do not want to get a disease. STDs range from annoying to life-threatening. Always protect yourself.

Finally, protect yourself emotionally. If you decide to do more than you are ready for, how will you feel when he sleeps with someone else? He will. Imagine him with someone else. If that would crush you, protect your heart. Your feelings guide you and his hormones guide him. Do not forget this. Ask your dad he will agree with me.

I remember being crushed when the guy I still liked broke up with me and got a new girlfriend. If I had gone further with him, I would have handled it much worse. That was probably my first heartbreak. Years later, I still had a crush on him. I never got him to like me again. I am positive that no physical action would change this. My past relationships help me relate to all of these pieces of advice that I share.

Chapter 3: Sometimes You Get Dumped

Boys will give reasons to let you down easy or dump you. Be aware of this. One big excuse is they will say that you are too nice or good for them. They will say they don't deserve someone like you. They are not trying to get you to convince them they are wrong. They are trying to dump you or let you down easy.

Freshman year in high school, my friend was going out with a boy. He broke up with her by telling her that she was too good for him and he didn't deserve her. He was just dumping her because he liked someone else. This is usually the case. We change our feelings about people a lot in our teens and lifetime. We can be totally in love and out of love with someone in the matter of a couple of months. Sometimes the other person is not over his or her feelings yet.

In my younger days, boys usually dumped me for another girl. This will happen a lot. Accept the dump and move on. You will like so many boys in your life. You will feel like your world is over at times. I promise it isn't. It is completely normal to have those feelings, we all do. Life is full of many ups and downs.

I don't have an interesting break-up story. Mostly I was just ghosted. This means that they just stopped calling. So that is a lot of fun. One boyfriend did that in adulthood. I was so shocked since I knew him for a lot of years. I just kept reaching out to see what the hell. I really wish I didn't do that. The minute he ghosted me and made excuses to stop emailing or calling, I should have walked away and held my head up high. It was his loss because I am a damn catch. I really mean it. Keep your head up and have confidence.

If you are getting the feeling that he is pulling away or that he is ready to end the relationship, then he probably is. Trust your intuition. Do not start panicking and try harder with the relationship. I did this. I thought reaching out and asking him what is going on would help. It did not. As soon as he stopped calling, I should have moved on, purely for pride. He did not change his mind and I could not change his mind. I think I was nervous because he was my first relationship after my long 4-year relationship. I remember being nervous that I would not find someone after I got out of the long-term relationship. Little did I know, your dad was waiting to tell me he liked me. Everything happens for a reason. I needed to date this other guy so your dad would be ready to ask me on a date.

Funny story, before I dated your dad we were friends. He was dating a girl and she broke up with him. He called me and asked me for advice on how to handle it. My advice was to tell her, "Ok." She made up her mind and broke up with him, there was nothing he could do but accept it and move on. He did not think that was great advice, but there was nothing he could do to change that girl's mind. So that is my advice to you. Accept it and move on.

I will not tell you that there are more fish in the sea. I will tell you that your heartbreak is temporary and you will feel better. Usually, the end of one relationship is so you can be open to a better one. He will not be the last love of your life. He will not be the last boy you love or the last boy to love you. This I am positive about.

The best way to handle a breakup is to accept whatever excuse he gives you. After you accept it, you can move on. By the time he dumps you, he has already moved on. Give yourself time to get over it. Accepting the end will help you heal quicker.

Next, make friend time a priority. Go out with your girls. See a chick flick, eat the ice cream, go to the mall. Come to me, I get it. I have been there and I remember all my young love boyfriends and breakups. Nana was amazing when this happened. She would be there for me and take me shopping. She knew it mattered to me and she treated it with that seriousness.

Don't forget to focus on yourself. Go back to the things that make you happy. Take an extra class for fun. Read a book, like this one.

Chapter 4: Cry with Family and Good Friends

    You will cry over a boy, it is ok. Just do not let him know you cried and don't cry in front of him. This is purely for pride. Your tears will not change his mind. Don't let him have the power of knowing he hurt you. My mom, Nana, told me this when I was young. I didn't believe her or think she knew what she was talking about, the same way you won't think I know what I am talking about.

    When someone stops liking you, he does not care about your feelings. So your tears will not have an effect on him. This is so hard to believe when your feelings haven't changed. Relationships are difficult. Your emotions will be real and intense. You will learn from them and grow.

Since your tears will not change his mind, do not give him anything that could embarrass you. Plus you do not want him to say that you were obsessed with him or call you crazy. Boys are not great at feeling emotions so they will deflect to make themselves feel better. If embarrassing you, takes the focus off of him, he may do that. Do not give them ammunition. Crying to the boy is desperate. It will not work so do not be the desperate one.

There is also this thing called the "ugly cry." When most people cry they are not attractive. You can see this again and again on reality television from the contestants of the Bachelor to the Real Housewives. Put your best face forward, and that is usually not the cry face. Save your tears for me. I will be there for you and hold you while you feel all your feels.

My mom was the best with this. She truly understood that teen love is deep and difficult. She treated any breakup with the seriousness of a grieving person's feelings. She would have a day with me, usually ended with shopping. I remember one breakup where I got new clothes and another where I got rollerblades.

You will break some hearts and others will break your heart. I will always be there for you. Your friends will be there for you too. Make sure you are there for your girlfriends as well. I will always let you cry to me. We can wear sweat pants, eat ice cream, watch chick flicks, and chill. These learning experiences are what help shape you and help you grow.

When my high school love dumped me, I was devastated. I cried and cried and thought for sure, if he knew I was upset then he would feel bad and still like me. Guess what- he did not. Then when my long term adult relationship ended, we both cried because it was over. It was not a desperate cry. It was a sad cry because we were together for a long time. It is sad when things end. There are differences in these two cries. Crying will not change the end result. So do not use the desperation cry. The sad cry is just natural.

Chapter 5: Your World is Bigger Than Him

When you have a boyfriend, you will feel like he is your whole world. When you are younger you feel so much more deeply. It is amazing and embrace it, but do not lose sight that he isn't your whole world. You are your own person and have your own life. Don't constantly ditch your friends for a guy. You will need your friends for so much longer. They will be there for you when your relationship ends. You may go through many different boyfriends while you are growing, that is ok. There will be relationships that make you think that it will last forever. Eventually one may, but I hope not until your late twenties.

The guy will not always ditch his friends for you, so if you are the ditcher you will be alone when he is gone. If he is always ditching his friends for you, then you both need to take a break. It is more than ok to let your boyfriend miss you and for you to miss him. Make sure you are well rounded and live for yourself.

My high school boyfriend was great. We had mutual friends so we were with other people a lot of the time. I had one friend that felt like I was ditching her for my boyfriend. I thought she was jealous since she didn't have a boyfriend. But she was just being honest and hurt that I wasn't there for her like before. I wish I could have seen that at the time. Side note, when a friend tells you something like this or anything, try to listen and reflect. Do not immediately get defensive. There is some truth in this and you have to recognize the part you are playing.

Odds are the boyfriend and you will break up eventually. You will want your friends to be there for you. If you ditch them for your boyfriend, they will not want to be there for you when your heart is broken. Friends are around much longer than guys. You and I just had this conversation. Girlfriends are so important. Be the friend that you want when your heart is broken.

As an adult, I need my girlfriends. We love and support each other. They will understand what you are going through since they are also girls. When given the opportunity, I chose girl time over date night. This is for my sanity. I did not realize how important my girlfriends were until I was older. Let me stress, they are extremely important.

I watch all of the Housewives. Some of these women are obsessed with having a boyfriend. I am thinking, why at 50 years old is this what you are most focused on. Focus on being successful and independent. Independent and strong women are the most attractive.

My mom raised me to be an independent woman. It is so important to have worth outside of your boyfriend or husband. Be proud of who you are. This means you find value in yourself. Accomplish things that you want. Play a sport, try out for a play, work on your degree, but most importantly love yourself.

How can you make sure you do this? One way is to say no to your boyfriend in order for you to hang with your girlfriends. Make sure there is time that is only for your friends. You don't have to invite your boyfriend to everything. The more your boyfriend misses you, the healthier your relationship will be.

Another way is to have your own interests. This is huge. I know I have already said this, but make sure you enjoy things outside of hanging out with the boyfriend. It may be hard to find out what you like. If you ever stop yourself from signing up for something because you will miss your boyfriend, then this is your clue to sign up for that thing. Do not limit yourself for the benefit of someone else. Take time to figure this out. I did not think about this enough earlier in life. I could not tell you that I had particular hobbies. I was not the most athletic. Nor did I have any talents or interests that kept my attention. Now, I enjoy reading, I love working out, and I love hanging out with my friends. I make sure I have time for these things now.

If you don't believe me read the book *Why Men Love Bitches* by Sherry Argov. This book explains all the ways to make sure you remain independent. It also shares how this is a very attractive quality.

Chapter 6: Give Your Boyfriend Space

Spending all your time with one person gets old. We as humans need breaks from each other. I love your dad and you kids, but I need breaks from you. You will get sick of friends at times and need breaks. The same goes for boyfriends. Again your emotions are so strong and heightened but too much time with one person isn't ever a positive thing.

You are way more appealing and attractive when you have your own life and things you do. If you have no idea what you like, freaking find something that you like. Ideally a physical activity or a sport are great ideas. Your body should be healthy and strong.

Do not pretend to be someone that you are not in order to get the guy to like you. Those girls are called "chameleon" girlfriends. It is ok to be open to learning and trying new things. That is healthy and will help you grow. Do not change who you are and what you like for someone else. Also, do not change all of your interests into your boyfriend's interests. You can start to like new things. Just do not give up *your* things. It is best to have your own likes that are different from your boyfriend.

Make sure you are social and have fun. Go out with friends, go to football, basketball, soccer, and hockey games. Have girl time without the boyfriends. Surround yourself with lots of friends. Some friends will be obsessed with their boyfriends because they don't have my great advice.

Do not spend every minute with your boyfriend. Sure it is fun and it feels great to be with the person you love. He will appreciate you more when you are not always readily available. Always being available is boring. It can lead to your boyfriend taking you for granted. Absence truly makes the heart grow fonder.

Here are some ideas on how to give your boyfriend space. Once a week, do something just for yourself, take a Zumba, yoga, photography, or painting class. If you are in sports, stick with that. Any of these will give you time to reflect and find yourself. You are more than someone's girlfriend.

Make sure you have friend time regularly. Make it a girl date. Maybe you can be the leader of these nights. Invite all your friends regularly. You can be the one that shares this with your friends. Not everyone will find it important at all times, but some will. It will catch on.

This will help you and your relationship. No one wants to feel smothered. This can help your relationship to last longer since it is healthier. You and your boyfriend will appreciate your freedom. Especially if you do not think you need time apart.

Chapter 7: Stay Away from Controlling Relationships

Lucky for me, I have never been in a controlling relationship. My worst abusive relationship is with Ben. (my son) He has been abusive since he was two. But in all seriousness, if it seems controlling or makes you feel less than, get the "eff" out. Those relationships are highly toxic and can cause a lot of damage.

If you are not sure if it is controlling, ask yourself does he tell you what to wear, tell you who to be friends with, or tell you to do anything? Does he get mad at you for going out with your friends?

Does he make you feel bad for hanging out with other people? This is not ok with a boyfriend or a friend.

Controlling relationships almost always turn abusive. If someone is like this, they have issues that have nothing to do with you. Maybe his parents had these issues, so he thinks all relationships are like this. You will never be able to help a boy that has controlling issues. People are capable of change if they truly want it and with tons of therapy. You are not a therapist nor should you try.

No one deserves to be treated this way. Stop investing in someone that does this. Get out early. Save yourself more pain and torture. Staying will cause you to lose self-respect. You will start believing you deserve it. This is no way to live.

One way to make sure this doesn't happen is to be open. Make sure you have a person to share things with. When they are worried about you, listen. If someone has concerns, take those seriously. You can always confide in me, but I hope you also find a close friend to share with. The friend will be around you more and may see things before I would.

If you feel like you have to hide things that he says or does, it isn't ok. This is your red flag. You already know this since you are hiding things. These relationships create patterns. If you accept it in one relationship, odds are you will accept it in more. Get out and take care of yourself.

If someone is concerned and talks to you about a relationship, you need to listen. You probably already know it, if your instinct is to lie. Do not make excuses for bad behavior. There just is not an excuse for this kind of behavior. I do believe there is a reason for every type of behavior, but that is not the same as an excuse. You may know the reason but you do not have to tolerate it. Nor should you, ever.

You already have grown up in a home that is not controlling. I have my own interests and friends and so does your dad. We always understand when we each have something to do. I still have my girl time and dad has his guy time. My mom and dad had this healthy relationship as well. I want to see you happy and in healthy relationships. Healthy relationships set the example for more healthy relationships.

Chapter 8: Keep Your Relationships on Social Media Light

I am in shock at how many adults are posting pictures of their new boyfriends on Facebook or Instagram, only to break up with them after. Give social media a rest. It does not need to be a place to showcase your love life, good or bad. Posting pictures too soon may scare the dude away. When you post about fights or reasons you are mad, people read it. Then it is hard to make people think your relationship is healthy after the public fight is over.

Your dad can be funny. He made a comment about a couple posting "Happy Anniversary" on Facebook. He said why did they post that, weren't they going to see each other today? It is so true. Social media is not the place to proclaim your undying love for someone. Keep social media cute and casual.

There was a New York Housewives episode where one woman tried on wedding dresses and she was not engaged. Reality TV is the ultimate social media. Her boyfriend clearly saw the episode, since it is on television. That does not look cute or casual. Putting such high stakes on a relationship is setting it up for failure. PS, they have broken up a few times since that episode. Shocking!

There are ways to avoid this epidemic. If you post a picture with your boyfriend, no need to write a long caption. There is no need to declare your love on social media. Keep your undying love off of social media. You can have all of these deep feelings but you don't need to blow up your news feed with them. People who do this tend to be pretending or trying to hold on to something that is over.

For every picture you post with your boyfriend, make sure you have an equal amount of nonrelationship posts. Your life needs to be larger than your relationship; your life and social media should show this. He should never be your whole world, so don't let social media think he is.

Dad and I do not post long sappy posts about our marriage. We also never go to social media with an argument we are having. No matter how private you make your accounts, it is out there and people can screenshot any post you make. Things you post will never truly go away.

I did not have social media as a teenager, I am truly grateful. I have witnessed young girls staking a claim on a guy. I am sure that is a strong motivator for making relationship posts. Pay attention to this.

Do not be the girl that has to stake a claim on a relationship. If you fear that someone else likes your boyfriend, let that fear go. It will not help you in any way. If someone likes you, trust that. If someone else likes him, so be it. You cannot change it so do not worry about it. Posting pictures of you and him will not make the girl like him less. Do not let that make you insecure. Take it is as a compliment that you have good taste.

Your boyfriends will change over the years or even months. You do not need to say that you love the new guy more than anything. You do not need to say that the guy is your whole world. It may feel like that but it is not true. No guy should be your whole world, even your husband. Your world is much larger than any one person. If it does not feel that way, you need to make a change.

All this being said, I did not get on social media until I started dating your dad. Thank goodness. When I was younger, I would have posted lots of relationship posts. I was lucky to not have social media in my life 'til later. You are not this lucky. You have been on my Facebook feed since you were born.

Chapter 9: Be Single in College

Don't expect a guy to be a boyfriend in college. They are so limited. They simply cannot handle the freedom and the opportunity to get as much ass as possible. I know you will wish it to be different, but the fact of the matter is, it will not be different. During that time of your life, you may meet a guy or two that you believe "is different," but they simply are not. Please have fun in college and have a strong group of girls. Be safe and smart. Guys will say and do anything that will help them get laid. Don't fall for it and you won't get hurt. Guys will do this most of the time, not just college time.

I didn't have one boyfriend in college, it may have been my braces, but doubtful. I have heard of girls having boyfriends in college, but those same guys were cheating on them at any opportunity. It is better to not have a boyfriend than to be the girl that is cheated on.

You will feel like you are ready for a relationship. Legally you are an adult. But you will change so much between your teens to your late thirties. This is a great time to explore your world. Save the heartache of a college relationship.

If you are in a relationship in college, you will feel like the next logical step is marriage. Pump the brakes; not yet. Learn what you like outside of the relationship. Read the next parts of this book to see what you can do instead.

Like I said, I did not have a boyfriend in college. I liked plenty of guys, but I am glad they were not boyfriends. I had a great group of girlfriends in college and I am still close to some of them.

Never assume that a hookup will result in a boyfriend. It simply will not. Guys rarely have anything else on their minds than hooking up. Sure they may think about sports, but they are not thinking about how fun having a girlfriend would be. Their brains are not thinking about romance, pretty much ever.

Chapter 10: Communicate What You Want

  I am actually adding this chapter because I told your uncle I was writing this book. He recommended that I add this chapter. Men do not think of these romantic ideas. Life is not a romantic comedy or a fairy tale. Life and relationships are wonderful but they are not like the movies. So do not hold your expectations to match the movies. It is not reality.

  I know it is romantic to think that a guy will sweep you off your feet. We like to believe that the right guy will do everything we could actually want. The reality is that we think differently and want different things. This is referred to as "love languages." What I mean is that what makes you feel special is not what makes him feel special.

Communication is hard in any relationship. The thing is that it is the MOST important thing in any relationship. Just because the boy does not show you the appreciation you want, it does not mean they do not appreciate you. You need to make things crystal clear. Beating around the bush or being passive-aggressive is never the way to go.

If you want him to plan a date, tell him that you would like him to take you out. If you want him to give you flowers, tell him you like flowers. Do not assume he is reading your mind. He is not. This goes both ways. He may prefer things that he is not saying. Opening that communication can help. It should also go like this, "I think we may find different things important, so I would like to share with you what I want and please share with me what you want."

This seems to defeat the purpose but it is so true. If you want something from him, say it. There is no chance that he is a mind reader or even that in tune to guess. Once you realize that this is true, expressing your feelings will be easier. Be willing to hear what he has to say also.

We have talked often about how gross boys are and that they do not change much as they get older. Your brother is obsessed with poop and farts. Your dad also thinks poop and farts are hilarious. Boys get older but they do not change much. They still laugh at references to anything disgusting. I cannot say "balls" at school without laughter. Even when I am talking about the kick balls. This is a perfect example of how people think differently.

I love your dad and I realize I have to tell him what I find important. I assumed for a while if it was important to him he would know it is important to me. This is not the case. One Mother's day he didn't get me a card or say anything. I had to tell him that it bothered me. I would like to get a card, I want to feel that he thinks I am a good mom. He just simply thought he has a mom and did not think of me since I am not his mom.

In return, he had to tell me that he needed me to be more understanding when it came to work. When you were born, it bothered me if he worked late. Before we had children, I never paid attention. He works hard and sometimes that requires times that are not the typical 9 to 5 hours. Now I am more conscious of this. It also helps that I work another job that requires me to work different hours as well.

Over 10 years ago this movie, called *The Break-Up,* came out. It is a story of a couple and their break-up. One scene shows the woman upset that the man didn't help clean up after they hosted a dinner party. She said you should want to help me clean. He responded that no one wants to clean. He is not wrong. No one wants to clean. The lesson is that the woman needs to communicate what she needs from the man. The whole movie shows the break down of their relationship. All could have been avoided if they communicated their needs and wants.

If you are a people pleaser like me, it will be hard to express your wants and needs. If you want any relationship to be successful, you need to be open and honest. In that same respect, you need to be understanding of the other person's wants and needs. I feel like I learn more about this everyday. Part of this is realizing that other people have other perspectives. They may look at situations differently than you. There is not a wrong or right way to look at situations, there are just different ways. Understanding this is helpful.

PART II: ADVICE for Dealing with Girl Friends

"Find your tribe and love them hard."- anonymous

Chapter 11: Understand Girls

Girls are much more difficult to deal with than boys. Girls are more emotional and they overthink things. I am guilty of this, in fact, I do not know one girl that is not this way. Plus all girls are different, this is really the huge factor. You will have the genuinely kind-hearted, the super selfish, the evil conniving, the jealous backstabber, the list goes on. I try to be a nice person but over my years of growing up, I have done all the above. Not proud of it and I have learned better for sure. I do have a great group of friends for which I am very lucky. Some of the girls I am closer to than the others but it is a great amazing group.

As you grow you will go through different emotions caused by hormones. While you are battling these changing and often extreme emotions, your friends are going through the exact same thing. You will find yourself angry and crying for no reason, other than it is that time of the month. Your friends will do the same. So you need to be aware of these irrational outbursts. When a friend is being irrational, hug them and know that it is coming from a totally unfair place. You will notice there are a lot of things that girls go through that boys would never survive. Make sure you always forgive these outbursts from friends. When you recognize that you do the same thing, it is easier to forgive.

Keep track of your cycle, start understanding when you are going through PMS. I know for me it is five days before I start. It sucks; it is not fun. Give yourself grace for dealing with this time. Don't use it as an excuse. Try to combat it with healthy eating and working out. Do things that make you happy during this time. Realize that no matter how you deal with it, it is still a factor.

Communicate this with your girlfriends. They may have not read this fabulous book so they don't have this leg up on life. Focus on honesty. When you are open and honest with your friends, they will be open and honest back.

Everyone perceives situations differently. Understanding this helps. You may not understand their perception but you can be aware that they have a different one than you. Knowing this will help you navigate relationships.

People have different experiences in life. These experiences shape them. You will share your life with all different people. Learning how to coexist in a healthy way is what relationships are all about. Everyone has a different family dynamic. I know when I was a child, I had friends that had different family lives than I did. I never realized how much these differences molded people to think and behave differently. I see this a lot now. Since I am a teacher, I meet at least twenty-five new families a year. Multiply this by my 18 years working in schools. All these families are so different. I have learned about this through training as a teacher.

As you grow you will change. Your friends will do the same. You will mature, but you will all do this at different times. Not everyone will mature at the same rate. This is another layer of relationships. Some people will never mature to the same point as others. I know plenty of adults that are self-centered, which is an immature trait. Life experiences can cause some to never fully mature. As you grow up, you are trying to figure life out. The secret is, no one has it all figured out. As you learn new things you continue to grow as a person. I am still growing right now in my life.

Then there is self-awareness. Many people do not self reflect. They are never aware of how they come across. No matter how many times someone tries to explain it, they will only see something through their perception. I do not mean this to sound judgmental. I do not have all the answers and I am sure I am not self-aware all of the time. My advice here is to try to see someone else's point of view. Do not always react on your personal feelings. Realize someone may be coming from a different angle. Again there is not a wrong or right, there are simply differences. You will not always agree with or understand someone's perspective. This is alright too.

Chapter 12: Try to Always Be Fair and Kind to Your Friends

Being fair with friends will take a lot of patience. I find girls to be more emotionally driven. Our hormones really do a number on us. Even at my age when I can rationally explain to myself what is causing this, it is still hard and I still go through all the highs and lows. Being empathetic means we can be accepting and give each other a break for our irrational moments.

Being kind to our friends takes self-reflection. We need to be aware of why we are feeling certain ways. Then we can express our feelings to our friends. There will be times you are upset and need a moment, letting our friends in on your feelings will help. They deserve to know that you are not upset with them. They will tend to think you are mad at them when you are not. Be careful to not blow up at your friends. Be aware of when you are crabby and share that so they know.

Up until recently, I took everything so personally. Turns out, most things are not about me. Crazy huh? My life has drastically changed for the better when I understood this. There are times I am on the brink of taking something the wrong way, and I talk myself out of it. I tell myself that it is not about me and get a grip. This usually helps.

When you are upset with a friend, try to see if it isn't possibly about you. Try to see where she is coming from. Everyone has different experiences that cause them to react the way they do. There will also be times when your friend has a different mindset or thought process that you will not understand or agree with. That is okay too.

Be kind even if the other person does not deserve your kindness. This is hard but so worth it. Do not let yourself dwell on a slight or an unkindness. It will do no one any good. I read good advice once before, "If it will not matter in 5 years, do not give it 5 minutes of your energy."

If we take every little thing so personally, we will always be unhappy. It is much more fun to be happy. This will take some effort to change your mindset. Once you do, it will become a habit. I would much rather look for the good in a situation than dwell on the negative.

There will be times when someone is not being nice to you. It happens. You will do the same at times. It is best to get over these times quickly. Dwelling on them will not help you in any way.

Another way to be kind to your friends is to not compete with them. Competing with friends sometimes is internal. This can be wanting to do better than your friend or wanting a boy to like you and not your friend. This is not a good look. Supporting each other is a much better way to go through life. When girls support each other they both rise. Cheer your friends on and be happy for their wins.

Chapter 13: Don't Let a Girl Friend Put You Down

Now that we covered hormones and emotions, we are on to mean girls. Sometimes girls will be jealous, vindictive, or just plain cruel. If you have a friend that is making you feel "less than," get out of that friendship. Turns out there are mean people out there. You do not need to surround yourself with them. I have had A LOT of experience with this.

In junior high, Jill and I were the targets of a lot of mean behavior. Girls that were my friends joined in on the attack. There were notes and comics written about us. I would get upset and I did not want to go to the same high school as them. Half went to my high school and the other half went to another one. Looking back on this, it was just mean. I couldn't blame it on hormones. One girl decided to be mean and others joined in on the fun. That is never ok. People will make mistakes and be mean, but when it is multiple girls against one or two, it is not OK. Do not ever join in the gang mentality. Be someone that helps others out.

Karma is real. What you dish out, you get back. Be careful you don't do this to others. Be the better person always. Be kinder than people deserve. Do not stoop to someone else's level and be mean. What goes around comes around every single time. You never have to worry about that.

Choose friends that are worthy of you and your friendship. You will have many different friends in your life. You will have childhood friends, then high school friends, college friends, work friends, and your kids' friends' parents. The good ones last a lifetime. Those are the best. I am lucky to have lifetime friends in my life.

If a so-called "cool girl" is the mean girl, walk away. I understand putting up with mean behavior so you feel like you belong, but it is better to be happy and healthy than to "belong." It is never cool to be mean, people that are mean are real losers and not worth it. Others who follow tend to be afraid of becoming the next target.

Most of the time the mean person is miserable with his or her life. They may have a bad home life. They may feel inadequate. They may be jealous. There is usually a reason for someone's behavior. That being said, it does not give someone an excuse to be awful. You do not have to accept this treatment, nor should you tolerate it. Like I mentioned before, it is not your responsibility to fix someone. The person needs to want to change and get help. This is a job for a therapist or a counselor.

You are never alone, even if you feel like you are. I remember feeling lonely during junior high. Everyone goes through it. You want to fit in, or feel cool. Look around and go to the support systems and old friends that are around you. Hang out with your totally cool mom. I mean for real, I am the coolest.

When Jill and I were the targets of mean girls, we had each other. We were each other's support outside of our families. Through this, we became closer and best friends. We went to high school together and had the best time. We made new friends and still talk about how much fun we had in high school. We went to football games, then we were the stat girls for the boys basketball team. Always look for the good friends. They are there for you.

Always look out for someone who is excluded. Be a good friend to everyone. You could literally change someone's life just by including him or her or being kind to him or her. This matters above all. Being kind is the coolest.

Chapter 14: Learn Which Friends You Can Trust

If you are anything like me, you are an open book. I am an "oversharer." I believe in being honest with who I am. But sometimes people will use that against you, or they will tell others. So you have to decide if you want everyone to know, if the answer is NO, then don't share.

Let's not worry about why someone would share your secret, let's just assume that they will. If it is something you don't want people to know, maybe don't share with anyone. It is ok to keep things private or just share with your family. The older you get, you will not worry about this as much. When you are in your teens, embarrassment is at the highest.

If someone betrays your trust, don't trust them again. You can continue to be friends, just be aware that secrets are rarely kept. The younger you are, the less likely friends will keep your secret. You will probably betray your friend's trust too. Try not to; no one likes a secret spreader. A lot of the times, secrets are spread to make the other person look better. The thing is, it doesn't make them look better; they just can't see it.

There will be things that you do not want the world knowing, so keep those private. Do not text or message any secrets. People can always screenshot it. If you do not want the world to see something, do not put it in writing or text. You may think the message is private and just between the two of you, but phones get left out and others can see it. You never know someone's intentions for using your words, but they can and sometimes do.

One time I wrote Jill a letter in college, this was before texting, and emailing was not big, either. She was having problems with her roommate. I wrote Jill, trying to cheer her up. The letter was not nice about her roommate. I told Jill she was jealous because she didn't have a boyfriend. Silly me never thought she would see it. Of course she did and we never were friends again. I get it now, it would be hard to see that written.

Just remember, keep things to yourself and out of text if you do not want the world to know. There is a saying to go by before you text, tweet, post, etc. T.H.I.N.K. It stands for Think if it is Helpful, Important, Necessary, or Kind. If not, do not do it.

Chapter 15: Don't Be Angry at a Friend for Talking Behind Your Back When You Have Done the Same

Friends will talk about you and you will talk about them. It won't always be a huge betrayal, so don't take it so personally. We all talk about each other. It is human nature. We all have opinions about each other. The older you get the more you realize you were not always right.

This is a hard one because with age you will care less. It gets easier the older you get. But maybe with this advice, you can start thinking with a different mindset now. The sooner you stop taking yourself so seriously, the happier you will be. If you hear something about yourself, assess if it is slightly accurate. If it is, then adjust your behavior. If it is not, who cares. Be like Elsa and Let it Go, or Taylor Swift and Shake it Off. The happiest people are the ones that can laugh at themselves.

Most of the time gossip comes from someplace else entirely. The gossiper could have PMS, or be in a fight with someone. People talk or gossip to make themselves feel better or less alone. It isn't ok, but you have the power to control your reaction to it. The less seriously you take this behavior, the less it matters.

Ways to protect your self include, keeping private things private. If you like someone and you do not want anyone to know, do not tell anyone. Not everyone intends on telling your secrets, but it happens. Just keep some things to your self. You can always share with me. I know better than to share your confidences. This also means not sharing your friends' secrets. If it is their secret, you do not have the right to share with anyone else. Not sharing your friends' secrets will also show the world that you can be trusted.

Talking about someone says way more about you than it does about the other person. I still struggle with this, but I am more thoughtful of this now. When I feel angry or upset, I try not to react right away. I would rather hold my head up high. There will be people that get under your skin. Sharing this and talking bad about them will not do you any favors. It is always better to be kind. Being nasty and negative is never a good look. Not everyone will see your point and then you look nasty. When you have gossiped, really think about it. Forgive yourself for doing it and focus on doing better.

Chapter 16: All People are So Different

Everyone has a different upbringing, background, and baggage. Not only are there differences, but everyone's perception of their life is different. Do not expect people to think the same way as you do. You may be the most rational person out there, it doesn't mean that others will think like you or that you can convince someone to see your point. Instead, try to see where someone else is coming from and go from there. When you realize you have a friend that will always think one way, don't try to change her. Life is easier that way. Either accept her for who she is or move on and find a different friend.

All my past and present friends are so different. We all think so differently. Different perspectives help us grow as humans. It is a good thing to have differences and different thoughts. Embrace and celebrate the differences. If everyone thought and behaved the same way, our world would be boring.

Expand your friendships. Find friends from all different backgrounds. Surrounding yourself with different people, will help you grow and see the world differently. Rachel Hollis says to make sure you surround yourself with friends that don't look the same. They should be from different cultures and have different experiences. Then you can truly see more perspectives. It is so important to see the world through someone else's perspective. The world is much bigger than your town, state, and country. It helps to see that and understand what that means to more people. Having a small mind is a great limitation. Open your mind and treat others with kindness.

Discussions and debates are great. While involved in one, listen to every person's point or perspective. Again their experiences shape their opinions. Make sure your experiences do not limit your opinions. You should always be accepting of other people, even if you don't share their opinions.

The older I get the more differences I notice. People have different passions, upbringings, educations, drives, motivations, desires, and relationships. All of these shape a person. There is no one perfect way to think or be. Always be accepting of other people. Remember you have no idea what wars, or battles someone is fighting. You will never know everything about someone. So learn to accept them. Two people who grow up in the exact same house and upbringing can be completely opposite. Everyone's perception of life shapes them.

Chapter 17: Be Judgment Free

It is human nature to judge. Really work on not doing that. Instead of judging your friends, decide to learn from them. It is hard to believe, but you will not always be right. We need to learn from others and accept our faults. By accepting your faults, decide to do better. What you don't like about someone else, do not become.

Eleanor Roosevelt said, "Great minds discuss ideas, average minds discuss events, small minds discuss people." Read this again. Now read it one more time. Let it sink in. It is a hard truth. I remember talking about people, thinking gossiping was fun and entertaining. When I did this I was small-minded. I thought I was the authority on their behaviors. This is not a good look. Discussing events is fine and average. Everyone participates. But you are more than average. Discussing ideas will contribute to your growth. People can do all three. Make idea-talking a larger part of your conversations than people-talking.

I think I get my gossiping fix from all my reality television. I am aware that it is my guilty pleasure. I get more than entertainment out of reality television, I actually study human behavior. I try to think why did that person behave that way. I know sometimes it is for more airtime, but sometimes it is not. Watching these shows taught me that sometimes people will never see that they are wrong. This helped me to walk away from situations where my words are not helping.

If someone has one narrow perspective, others cannot always widen it. I have tried and failed, to the point where it is almost comical. I want you to be open-minded and have a great mind. Not everyone will; some people are small-minded. This is where discussing ideas come into place. If someone has a fixed mindset they will more than likely be small-minded. You cannot change a fixed mindset, they have to want to change. Remember everyone is capable of anything with a growth mindset.

To stay away from judgment, choose to look for the positive in everyone. Everyone has something to offer. No one is all good or all bad. Give people the benefit of the doubt. Maybe they are having a bad day or going through something hard. Judging is not kind. You will want the same grace from people someday.

Chapter 18: Travel with Your Girlfriends Before Settling Down

    I did a lot of traveling in college and my early twenties. This is huge and helps with personal growth on different levels. A great reason to travel is because it is fun! I have so many memories of traveling with different girlfriends. Girl trips bring girls closer together. In college, we would visit a friend's sister. She lived in Florida. We traveled there on Spring Breaks, Fall Breaks, and Summer Breaks. We went to amusement parks. We went to spring training baseball games. We got to hang out with baseball players. It was a cool time and filled with awesome experiences.

    After college, I traveled to Key West a few times with girls. Life is expensive but save money to travel to fun places. Key West is a great time. We used Priceline and stayed at different places. Key West is fun and small. So no matter where you stay you are not far from Duval Street and the action. I was quite the karaoke star at that point. I learned that gazpacho was a cold soup, when I ordered it for a cheap dinner. It was not delicious. I also bought a pair of shoes that turned out to be two different colors. One was faded from being in the window. Of course I didn't realize this until I was already wearing them. So as you can see, you learn from traveling.

If you ever get a chance or an invitation for a girl's trip make it happen. In early adulthood, I was invited on a couple trips with girls. The trips were work trips for them and they were able to extend it through a weekend. I was able to go to Vegas and Miami inexpensively. Both trips were in style and so much fun. We stayed at awesome fancy hotels. We went to the coolest clubs. We ran into celebrities, this was right up my alley.

These trips and experiences are key. Before you settle down and have a family, it is important to have fun and this type of freedom. Having this time will make you happier. You won't feel like you missed out on anything. It is so important to do things that make you happy and fulfilled.

When I started teaching, we took a few spring break trips to Vegas. This bonded me to these life long friends. The memories and stories are beyond funny. We thought we were the funniest. I am pretty sure we kept a notebook of our funny quotes and stories.

Your girlfriends will be your sanity as you grow older. You will realize you need them and count on them more than you thought possible. Enjoy them and have fun together.

Once you have a family, continue your girl's trips. They may look different, like weekends away at a winery or a night in the city. These trips are amazing and will give you the time you need for yourself.

Your life will go through different seasons. Getting out there and doing things that you enjoy are important. Reading back on my trips, you can tell what I enjoy. I love trips that include the sun and fun. Find what you enjoy. You may prefer mountains and lakes, culture and history, or cruises and excursions. Whatever you prefer, make sure you get out there and do that.

The world is a big place. You owe it to yourself to explore it. If there is a place you are dreaming of traveling to, make it happen. Start saving for the trip. Travel is one thing you can spend money on and it actually makes you richer. Experiences are always better than material things.

Part III: Advice for Life

"Look closely at the present you are constructing. It should look like the future you are dreaming."- Alice Walker

Chapter 19: Always Be Kind

Being kind is huge. I would prefer people to be kind over rich, smart, popular, etc. In everything you do, show kindness. This can look like a lot of different things.

Being kind at work or school means always offering a smile. Everyone is battling something, your smile could turn around their day. At work or school, people are typically stressed and have their minds running a mile a minute. Just smile and say hello. Not everyone will be receptive or notice, but it is always better to be kind.

Be kind to strangers. You can do this all of the time. Hold the door for someone at a store. Offer to pay for someone's coffee. Random acts of kindness have a ripple effect. You don't need to see all of the good it has done, but you can be proud that you started something. Think of a time when you were upset or having a bad day, now picture yourself at Starbucks for a treat and the person in front of you pays for your drink. It would turn around your day.

Be kind to acquaintances, even kinder than people deserve. You do not have to treat people the way they treat you. You can show kindness and grace. This is a much harder thing to do. You do not have to let people mistreat you, but you do not need vengeance. The world will work itself out. Karma is real and she is a bitch.

Be kind to those closest to you. The people to which we are closest sometimes hurt us the most. They need your grace and kindness. I once read that people who need love the most, show it in the most unloving ways. Their behavior probably has nothing to do with you. Give your people space and come back at a later time and see if you can help or find out what is wrong. We sometimes take out our frustration on those closest to us. Try to be conscious that you may be doing this to those you love. Be aware that the people you love may unfairly take things out on you.

When I am crabby, I am the crabbiest with your dad. We share a life and he gets the brunt of my emotions. I try to keep them to myself but they still come out directed at your dad.

My best advice for this is, to be honest. Whenever I am crabby, I try to warn my class that I am in a bad mood. Their actions will intensify my mood. I will try and tell you and Ben when I am crabby as well. Giving someone the heads up will help them to not get upset with you.

Chapter 20: Choose Work That Makes You Happy and Try Your Best

You will need to work to make income and build your life. There will be jobs that are strictly for the money. There are other jobs that turn into your career and passion. Put your all into any work and enjoy the fact that you are earning. Switch your perspective of your situation. Look for the good that you are contributing. If you work at a store, offer smiles and kind words to customers. If you wait tables, be the best server. Make someone's dining experience memorable.

When deciding where your life will lead, really look at what you enjoy. Find a career that allows you to enjoy working. If you find yourself in a career you are not enjoying, figure out a way to get out of that job. Life is short and you work the majority of your life. Be happy and enjoy the work you are doing.

I didn't go to college to be a teacher. My first degree is in advertising. After college, I could not find a job. I did not know where to begin. My advice is to do different internships to see what you like. After college, I started subbing in schools. Then I realized I wanted to be a teacher, so I went back to school. Now here I am a teacher and an entrepreneur. You should also figure out ways to earn multiple streams of income. According to Forbes, millionaires have an average of seven streams of income.

You need to put effort into anything you do. While in school, pay attention and work hard. You can't grow in life if you are not learning. Keep learning and continue to improve. Even when you are 39 and old like me. I recently went to a conference. The CEO said if you are not growing you are dying. Life long learners are the most successful and the happiest.

To be valuable at work, do more than is expected. Too many people will just do their perceived requirements. Those people do not get promoted or valued. My biggest pet peeve is laziness. To be successful, go the extra mile. It will pay off, I promise. There is a fabulous book called *The Slight Edge* written by Jeff Olson. This little extra you contribute is the "slight edge" that puts you ahead. Read this book when you are done with my book. When you continue to try your best and work harder than is expected, this behavior becomes a habit. This is a healthy habit to begin.

I recently read a quote that means so much. "A formal education will make you a living, self-education will make you a fortune." This is so true. Keep learning and growing. Be the best at whatever you pursue. Another stat I read said that millionaires say they read at least 30 books a year. I am not there yet, but I am reading more and more. I continue to learn and grow. This is opening my mind and increasing my income. I have big goals and dreams and I am determined to reach them. If I didn't read and continue to learn, I would not think these dreams were possible. I would not be writing this book.

I love my jobs and am truly happy going to work and working from my phone. I am off in the summer and I choose to work my business. I think this is a huge accomplishment. Many people are unhappy and just go through the motions of work. They live for the weekend or vacations. This is sad to me because you spend the majority of your life working. It is so important to love what you do. My dad always told me that if you love what you do, you will never work a day in your life.

Chapter 21: Keep Social Media Positive

    I am guessing social media will still be a thing when you are older. It keeps growing. Focus on keeping negative comments and complaints off social media. No one is drawn to a negative complainer. Crabby people only bring more crabby people to them. When I see someone post vague complaining posts, I am turned off. I tend to unfollow people who do that. How does it make you feel when someone complains all of the time? I am guessing not good.

    If you focus on being positive on social media, you will probably keep negativity and complaining out of your life. We tend to behave like the 5 closest people to us. So surround yourself with positive people and live a happy life. If your close friends are negative, maybe you can be the positivity that they need. People are genuinely drawn to positive people.

It is easy to be negative and complain on social media when you are reading negativity all the time. If you see certain that people are always bitching, hide their posts. You will feel happier for it. Once you stop seeing all that complaining, you will not feel the need to join in the complaining.

This is not something new. I know you have heard it before. But really reflect on the people you enjoy being around. What do you like about their company? How do you feel in their presence? What qualities do you admire? I can guarantee it is not negativity.

Keeping social media light also means not comparing yourself to someone else. If you see someone else's posts and they make you feel jealous or angry, stop following them. You should never compare yourself to someone else. Do not overthink other people's posts. Understand that people mostly post the best things. Focus on positivity. Instead of hating on someone else for having things that you want, cheer others on.

Focus on all the things you should have to be grateful for. One way I do this, is by writing down at least 10 things I am grateful for each day. They can be simple things like Ben smiled this morning. Keeping track of your gratitude will force you to focus on the positives of life. No matter what is going on, you can always find some reason to be thankful.

Chapter 22: Keep Politics and Religion Out of Social Functions

My dad told me that his parents gave him advice that he should not talk about religion or politics at social functions. This advice is huge. If someone is passionate either way, they will not be convinced otherwise. The Trump presidency is a huge reminder that people are divided. It is really hard to hear people and their opinions, especially if they are not your opinions.

Just because you don't agree with someone on politics or religion, it doesn't mean you will not get along. There are a lot of reasons you will befriend people. It is nice when you have the same beliefs and core feelings, but it isn't everything. Other people's opinions may teach you something about people.

Your beliefs will grow and evolve while you do. In my early adulthood, I believed one way and the older I grew, I went the opposite way. Your job and career will make you support certain politicians. I advise that you educate yourself, and know who you should support. Your support and beliefs are no one's business.

There are people in my life that like to talk about politics all the time. Mostly, because they like to get a rise out of others. This kind of conversation is never productive. Stay away from it. Think what you want and move on. Engaging in these conversations will upset you unnecessarily.

When you are figuring out what you believe, you will need to hear different perspectives. The world is changing and I would guess there will be three major political parties in the future. There is a new perspective that is neither all conservative nor all liberal. The independent voice is becoming more prominent. Just remember you will disagree with people. You will not get them to change their minds. So do not try. Thinking you can convince people to see the world the way you do, is exhausting.

If someone is trying to engage in a political or religious debate, you have a couple of options. You can decline politely. You can change the subject. You can politely excuse yourself. The other option is to engage, but that usually leads to heated debates or anger. My advice is to stay away. I wish I would engage less.

Chapter 23: Do Not Be a Doormat

I think it is important to be kind to people and do things for others without expectations of anything in return. That being said, do not constantly do for others if they are just using you. This will look different in all different stages of life.

Don't ever do someone's homework or work for them. This can never end well. It isn't really helping the person. Friendships should be equal. So if you are the one doing all the work or effort, you need to recognize this. I believe I am usually naïve when meeting people. It takes me longer to recognize someone who is out to gain something. It never feels good once I figure it out.

Helping others is what we all need to do. Please don't confuse what I am saying. If you are always helping the same person, over and over, you are being taken advantage of. There are givers and takers. Strive to be a giver, but make sure that it isn't always to the same taker.

It's ok to let a friend pay for you, but make sure you return the favor. Also, make sure you are not always the one paying for everyone.

This applies to emotions as well as money. There will be takers in your life that just take all your energy. You do not have to give all your energy to others. It is harder to recognize this type of giving. You think you can be a shoulder to lean on without giving too much. This emotional drain can be worse and more harmful than a financial drain.

There was a cool quote that I read. "You do not have to set yourself on fire to keep another warm." It means helping others should not be to your detriment. I am realizing that I cannot be a good mom or teacher if I don't practice self-care. An empty vase cannot share any water. If I am stressed or exhausted, I am of no use to anyone else. This is a reminder to do things for yourself. Fill your own cup first.

You can not be everything to everyone. It feels good to be needed and it feels good to do things for yourself. This does not make you selfish. You need to find the balance of both.

If a situation or person does not enrich you or lift you, you need to remove yourself. When you are out of the situation, you need to reflect on how you got there. You do not want to make this a pattern. You should never tolerate cruel or berating behavior from anyone. If others are warning you, you need to really listen.

Chapter 24: Laugh at Yourself Often

When you take yourself too seriously, you are opening yourself up to unnecessary hurt. We are all human and fallible. The quicker you accept that, the happier you will be. We all make mistakes, we all fart, we all burp, we all embarrass ourselves. Own it and laugh at it. Laugh with others even at your own expense. Finding humor in most things, helps a lot. This also leads to having a good sense of humor.

When you accept this truth, you will not be so sensitive. Taking things too personally will only cause you pain. Assume someone's actions have nothing to do with you. This helps when being sensitive or upset.

I am sensitive when it comes to watching movies, or hearing heart-warming stories. I cry so easily. You laughed at me for crying over a Junie B. Jones book. But I decided to not be sensitive when it comes to me. More often than not, having hurt feelings comes more from a misunderstanding.

I love this quote from Rachel Hollis, "Someone's opinion of you is none of your business." This is so true. If someone doesn't like you, oh well. It is their loss. Not everyone will like you, there is not much you can do about that.

Being self-reflective will help. You really need to look at yourself and see why you are hurt. Is it embarrassment, feeling disrespected, not understood, etc. Then look at what drove the person's actions. Was that other person thinking of you or your feelings? Is the action even about you? Why are you upset that they didn't consider your feelings? Is it possible the other person doesn't even know you are upset? Are you willing to communicate your feelings? Do you prefer the pity and feeling sorry for yourself? Will it matter in 5 years? If not, don't give it more than 5 minutes of your time. I love this advice. I also like the advice of sleeping on it, do not make permanent decisions based on immediate emotions. Give yourself time to process your feelings.

Eventually, you will get to the point where you do not care what others think of you. It usually comes with maturity and age. Since you are going to get there eventually, train yourself to get there sooner. Your life will get easier quicker. This took me a long time to understand. I would take things personally most of the time. That does not help, ever.

Just because you do not take everything so personally, it does not mean that others won't. If you have friends that are more sensitive, be aware and try to see what is bothering them. Feel free to share this book or this chapter with friends that take things more personally. This goes back to the chapter that explains that everyone is so different.

Chapter 25: Live on Your Own Before You Live with a Boy

You will live with us and one day you will not. Do not go from your parent's house to living with a boyfriend. You should be more independent than that. You will depend on your parents for the majority of your life, and that is fine. I still depend on my parents. They help with you kids so much. But don't go from depending on your parents to depending on a guy to take care of you. Learn to take care of yourself.

Many times people think they will save money by living with their significant other. Living on your own is a lot of fun. It is cheaper to have a roommate. So have a roommate, not a live-in boyfriend. Living with someone is work. It will make your relationship less romantic. Sleepovers are fun, traveling with boyfriends is fun, but living with someone is work. I promise you.

I didn't live with a boyfriend. This is for the best. There was one time when I almost did. It would have been a disaster. Our relationship ended soon after this time. I lived with your dad for two months before we got married. That was simply because my condo in the city sold. Dad and I were planning a wedding and already combining our belongings at this point.

I have tried to pass this advice on and it is not taken. I realize much advice is not always received. People have to learn for themselves. I do not know one person that regretted living on her own before marriage. I enjoyed living in the city. Being downtown was so much fun. Other friends of mine shared apartments first. They always enjoyed this time. College roommates do not count. Live with girlfriends after college. These experiences are priceless.

Learn to pay your bills and budget money. Life can change in an instant, have skills to get you through any ups and downs that life can bring. When I hear a woman say they don't know how to pay the bills, I want to shake them. Everyone should know how to pay the bills. You are responsible for your life.

Learn to take care of small household things, plunging a toilet to changing a toilet seat. Paint your walls, hang pictures or mirrors. It feels good to be able to do this. News flash, all the directions to these tasks are on YouTube. You can search anything and watch a video on how to accomplish the task. You will have a sense of accomplishment from completing these small household issues.

Having this independence will also give you the strength to handle things that life throws at you. Nothing is guaranteed in life. People get sick and leave. I want you to be strong to handle anything in life. As long as I am living, you will not be alone. I just want you to be mentally strong enough to handle life. The world will throw you curveballs. Gather your strength and tackle it. Sometimes the bravest thing we can do is to ask for help. So knowing where to find the help is a skill in itself. Do not ever depend on someone else to carry you through life. You are my daughter. You are strong, capable, and smart. I have all the faith in the world that you can handle life. If I can do this life, so can you!

Chapter 26: Stay Classy and Educated on Social Media (and In Public)

This is something I say to my students all the time. Stay classy and educated. Whatever you post on social media is there for the whole world to see, no matter how private your account is. If you wouldn't want your parents or a potential employer to see something, do not post it. My grandma told my mom to never put anything in writing that you don't want the whole world to see. The same goes for posting on the Internet, even more so.

People who make mean comments online are called Trolls. No one wants to be labeled a troll. Being mean is not classy or educated. It goes against being kind, which is my most important rule that I hope you follow.

What you put out on social media is who you are. You should be authentic. People are always watching, show the world who you are. Be good, kind, fair, classy, and educated. What you put on Facebook could cost you friends, jobs, scholarships, and peace. Social Media is not some small private group, it is larger than your little world. Things do not go away. Your potential college or employer can see any stupid thing you put out there.

Your friends' parents can see this. Do you want them to see this? Would they want you to be friends with their children if they saw your posts? Would you want me to see this? If the answer is No, DO NOT POST IT.

There is a classic acronym for posting or speaking. THINK. T- Is it true? H- Is it helpful? I- Is it interesting? N- Is it necessary? K- Is it kind? If it is not all 5, do not post it. Be someone that you can be proud of. Keeping your social media clean will help you here.

I did not have social media until I was 27. Thank goodness for this. I did not have it because it did not exist when I younger. Well, friends of mine were even older when they started using social media. One friend did not get hired for a job because the potential employer saw his Facebook profile. This friend was in his thirties. So if my friend did not get a job as an adult, then imagine what you could miss out on if you do not have a clean social media account. There are stories of high school students losing scholarships because of social media.

Cameras are everywhere. Everyone with a smartphone has a camera, yet another newer thing. My first cell phone did not even text. I had to have a phone and a digital camera. Everything is in one device now. So if cameras are everywhere, you have to be careful of what you are doing. You never know who is taking a picture and posting it. Be kind and do the right thing. This will help you in situations. Always assume that whatever you are doing can be recorded and added to social media. Because it will probably be on someone's phone.

Chapter 27: You are Not Better Than Anyone and No One is Better Than You

We are all human and have something incredible to offer. Treat everyone you come in contact with respect. Someone's job or career does not make them above or below you. Our world needs everyone working together to keep our world clean, safe, and cohesive.

Some people think they are above others because of their education or money. This means nothing in life. People's value is not determined by their diplomas or wealth. Work hard and be happy with your work. Anyone can accomplish anything they desire if they work at it. If you are teachable and are determined to grow, you will.

I have heard many people say they are just going to be... They have resigned themselves for a mediocre life. This is not true. I hope to share this knowledge with everyone. Do not let anyone tell you that you cannot do something unless I am telling you no to something. But otherwise, if you have a dream, reach it.

I am a teacher, and teachers are not known for having high paying salaries. I used to think, that is fine. I decided to be a teacher, so I decided to not make much money. I would sometimes sit there and think, what if I was a lawyer or a doctor. Neither of these professions appealed to me, but I figured that was the only way I could make a lot of money. Then I saw friends selling things online through network marketing. I really did not know that much about it. When I found my side hustle, I just decided to go for it. Why not, what do I have to lose. The answer is absolutely nothing. At the age of 37, I started my business. I thought that it would be nice to make a couple hundred a month. It turns out that this is exactly what I needed in all aspects of my life. I started reading more to learn more. These books changed my views on life. I gained a new community of women that support each other. I have inspired other women to go for things. I mentor women on my team and my cross line teams. Because of this chance I took, I decided to write a book. Through trainings I have done, I took a training in self-publishing a book. I am not too old to try something new the same way no one is too young to try something. Do not let age, inexperience, or anyone deter you from reaching a goal.

You will come in contact with thousands of people in your lifetime. Every person you meet has been put into your life for a reason. We learn from everyone. Some people will teach us compassion, while others teach us humility. Every person has value, make sure you see this. Every relationship will teach you something. Reflect on relationships and see what they can teach you.

My first adult relationship taught me a lot. I was subbing and going back to school to be a teacher when we started dating. He was 6 or 7 years older than me and he was going back to school to be an orthodontist. We met through my best friend and her boyfriend. Because he was going through school, we only saw each other on the weekends. We dated for 4 years. During that time, I moved to the city and we lived close to each other. He was still so busy with school, that I had time to focus on myself. I used this time wisely. I was starting my career as a teacher. So I got my Master's Degree, during this relationship. I had moved all the way up the pay scale before I was married and had you. This helped me so much.

If I did not have this relationship, I may have fallen into the trap of focusing my attention on my boyfriend and not myself. I may not be the independent strong woman that I am today. I am fortunate enough to recognize this and that I did have the opportunity to focus on myself.

Chapter 28: If You Do Not Like Something, Do Not Become It

There will be times when you are totally turned off by someone else. There will be other times when people annoy you. Remember these actions and work ultra-hard to not do these actions yourself. When you recognize behavior that you do not like, reflect on yourself to see if you do these same offenses.

If you can't stand when people complain, then don't be a complainer. Negative people and complainers are the worst. I really try to make sure that I am not spreading negativity. Last night I saw a friend's post on Twitter. She shared a quote, "Talking about our problems is our greatest addiction. Break the habit. Talk about your joys." This is powerful and so true. Once you start complaining, you continue it just like a habit or addiction.

I cannot stand meanness. Sure there are times that I would like to be mean to someone who is being mean to me or others I care about. It makes my blood boil when people are being rude or mean on purpose. Everyone has a bad day or moment, the key is to not take it out on others. They don't deserve it and you don't deserve to feel guilty later. Before you do anything, ask yourself if it is kind. If it isn't kind just don't do it. You will not feel better by getting revenge. You will feel worse for stooping to that level. Hold your head up and be proud of being kind.

I have distanced myself from friends because of negativity. It happened kind of naturally. While it was happening, I did not even realize it. Then I became more self-reflective. Why did I keep in contact with some people more than others? It turns out that I was separating myself from constant negativity. These people are not even aware of how negative they are. I have actually heard them say that they dislike complainers, when that is all they do. Over the years I thought, if I just could tell them how they come across, they would change. Turns out that did not work either. Not everyone can see how he or she come across. I am sure I come across a certain way that I am not aware of either. My goal is to be a positive person and choose happiness. So if that is annoying, I am ok with that.

Learn to be self-aware. Ask others how you are perceived. Be willing to take constructive criticism. This will help you grow as a person. I do not believe anyone is done growing. There are always new things to learn and accomplish, at any age. The world is constantly changing, people need to adapt to these changes. Be open and willing to learn.

Chapter 29: Don't Make Excuses

Excuses will get you nowhere and nowhere quickly. At times you may have reasons for not reaching a goal. Look at why you didn't reach the goal and change your behavior, do not accept the excuse. Life is not always easy and obstacles will occur. If you really want something, go after it and do not quit.

I am currently teaching third grade and I have a side gig. I sell shampoo with network marketing. I love this experience and challenge. I am committed to rising in this company. I am not where I would like to be at the moment but I am not stopping. I am taking workshops and educating myself. I am also reading a lot of personal development books. These are key to stopping the excuses.

Your mindset will help you accomplish everything that you want to achieve. Believe in yourself and work hard, excuses will not help. I love this quote from author Jen Sincero, "You can have your excuses or you can have your success. You can't have both." No truer words have been spoken. It is ok to fail, we learn from failure. We learn nothing from passing the blame on someone or something else. Look at the happiest people you know. Look at what makes them happy. It is not material things; it is their mindset. I bet they focus on what is going right in life, not the negativity. Look for the positive outcomes, negativity breeds more negativity.

I see too many people making excuses for why they cannot do something. If you really want something, you will find a way. If you want to run a marathon, you will train. If you want to lose weight after having children, you will be conscious of what you are eating. If you want to save money, you will stop spending and make a budget. If people worked as hard on their goal as they do on making excuses, they would reach their goal.

As I write this chapter, I gave myself a goal on when I want to finish this book. I said by the time that I am forty. Well, that is just around the corner. I am great at setting goals, and I am also great at working at the last minute. Rachel Hollis gave great advice, you can do anything you want just one thing at a time. She talked about carving out time each day to write so she could finish her book. I love this and have to push myself to do the same thing. It is easy to let other responsibilities deter you from goals. Make promises to yourself and keep them.

Chapter 30: Protect Yourself

This is an important chapter for girls. Our lives are a tad different than the boys here. We are more vulnerable and have to fear for our safety more. There are a few ways we need to protect ourselves more than men. We need to have more protection around drinking and physical situations.

While drinking, we need to remember moderation. I know that it sounds lame and you know this. Drinking can heighten emotions. Before drinking, know your headspace. These emotions will not be dulled when drinking. They will be exaggerated. If you are struggling with something, drinking will depress you. If you aren't in a good headspace, be the designated driver that day.

When drinking, your instincts are dulled. Make sure you are in a safe place while drinking. Use the buddy system, this means make sure no one leaves alone. People can and will take advantage of you if you are too drunk. You should not drink until you are legal. There are too many laws and consequences for this. I have seen kids lose scholarships or lose their positions on a sports team for drinking underage. It is not worth it, I promise.

Another way to protect yourself is to not put yourself in potentially dangerous situations. I know this makes sense but sometimes we don't think beforehand and we also trust people when we should not. I was thinking what tangible advice can I share for this and I came up with it. Before you will be alone with someone, decide whether or not you would mind kissing him. If the answer is no, do not allow yourself to be alone with him. You cannot trust that a guy won't want to try something with you, even if he is a friend. Just because you think someone is cute, doesn't mean it is ok for him to force himself on you. The best way to be safe is to stay away from these settings.

In these situations, you cannot worry about other people's feelings. I know sometimes we worry about people's feelings. We don't know how to tell them no or that we are not interested. Well as I get older I hear too many stories of girls being forced to do things. Eff his feelings. Your safety will always be more important than a guy's feelings. The fact that you even have to deal with this, pisses me off. Girls are at the disadvantage here, so keeping yourself protected will keep you safer.

When I was in college, I was a server at a restaurant. One night, I needed a ride home from work. Everyone was going to hang out together, I just needed to go home first. A guy that I worked with offered to drive me home. I was twenty-one and my guess is he was around forty. We worked together and everyone knew him, so I did not think anything about it. When he drove me home, he tried to kiss me. Now it was as disgusting as it sounds. I was twenty-one and he was around forty. I got out of the car quickly and I felt really gross. It is not fair that I had to feel gross or bad for not wanting to make out with this guy. I know I was lucky that nothing else happened, but it still sucks.

You do not owe anyone anything physically ever. Never feel bad for this. It is insane that men feel entitled to anything physically. How could this forty-year-old think a twenty-one-year-old would be interested? Protect yourself by not being alone in these situations. Make sure you are always with a friend. Wait for rides even if it is not convenient. Stay on the phone with someone if you have no other choice.

Chapter 31: Live in the Moment

I used to be terrible at living in the moment. While I was on vacation or doing something fun, I would always think about what is next. When I focused on the next thing, I didn't enjoy the moments that I experienced. I noticed that focusing on the next thing made me feel anxious. Feeling anxious is not a great feeling.

It is easy to let life become a routine. Many people dread Mondays and weekdays. Again this is not living. Live for today; enjoy all the moments. Create a life that you are excited to live. Practice gratitude; get a journal and keep track of things you are grateful for every day. Focus on the positives and things that went well. When something goes wrong, focus on what you can learn from that experience.

We started the tradition of going to dinner with Gampie on Mondays. We love these days with each other. It is one reason to be excited for Mondays. So start a Monday tradition.

When I slow myself down, I learn to soak in the good vibes and experiences. Someone told me to take mental pictures and soak in all the fun on my wedding day. I followed that advice and enjoyed every minute of my wedding. Then I took this advice and applied it regularly. It helps me enjoy more things.

I am now applying that advice to everything. Sitting by a pool in the summer, cozying up with a blanket on a cold day, watching my kids play at every age. This piece of advice has led me to be happier person. Look for the positive in every situation. Always have gratitude for what you have.

Still continue to make goals and crush them, but enjoy all the little moments along the way. When you realize this life is wonderful, you see everything through happiness. Your happiness is the most important thing you can possess.

Choose to accept invitations that make you happy. Surround yourself with people you enjoy. My favorite saying is, "Live your best life." My biggest wish for you is that you are happy, I mean truly happy. When you are happy, you realize that you are living your best life.

Deciding what makes you happy can be fun. Don't be afraid to try new things. Accept invitations to new experiences. When you find what makes you happy, make sure you get opportunities to do it. Don't put your happiness on the back burner. Your happiness is just as important as the people around you. There is nothing better than being happy.

Acknowledgements

I want to start my thank-yous with my inspiration, my children. Elle and Ben give me a new purpose in life. You are the reason I get to be a mother; I am truly blessed. My children amaze me every day. I hope you accomplish everything you dream. My biggest hope for you is that you are happy.

I need to thank my own mom, Mary Beth Palka. Without you, I wouldn't be the woman I am today. You raised me to be strong and independent. You have proven that women can bust through any glass ceiling by working hard. You are an inspiration to many, but I am the lucky one that gets to call you Mom.

My dad, Don Palka, has also made me into the woman I am today. Although I am not done relying on his help, he has taught me that I can figure it out. He has offered me a lot of advice and wisdom that I am practicing and sharing. I am so thankful that my parents raised me in a loving, happy home. This above all, has made me into a happy, strong, and caring person.

Of course I need to thank my husband, Mike Larson. He always supports me. When we were dating, he was proud that my class was in the newspaper. When I started my own business, he only offered words of support and encouragement. When I told him that I was writing this book, he said, "Ok." He has never laughed at me, only with me. His support and love mean more to me than he knows.

I need to thank my amazing friends. When I say they are amazing, I mean they are truly the best anyone could hope to find. They have always supported me and lifted me in ways only friends can. We share our lives, families, annoyances, excitements, dreams, doubts, fears, and hopes with each other. We solve world problems, and live our best lives. My world would have a huge hole without them. Thank you, Sara, Jill, Bridgett, Kimberly, Jeannie, Christine, Karrie and many more.

Without this girl, I wouldn't have followed this series of events that led to this book. Thank you Amanda Broomhead. Your support and encouragement are more than appreciated. If it were not for you, I would not have started my own business. If I did not start my own business, I would not have met the next person I need to thank.

Kimberly Olson, thank you for all your education and training. You have taught me a lot about business and reaching goals. You inspired me to write and showed me how to self publish. Thank you for being a mentor.

I want to thank Anna Barefield. Thank you for editing my book. Thank you for loving it and giving me the confidence to complete it.

Finally, I want to thank Antonia Marie Photography for the stunning cover picture. I appreciate your work and accommodating us so quickly.

Made in the USA
Las Vegas, NV
02 March 2024

86608798R00060